# Belair Early Years Science

Jea**ns**

# Acknowledgements

The author and publisher would like to thank the headteachers, staff and children of Whinney Banks School Foundation Unit and Darlington College Early Years Centre for their invaluable help in the production of this book. A special 'thank you' goes to Sue Welburn, Hayley Hughes and Andrea Cartwright for their very kind support in the setting up of the displays for this book.

**On Reflection (page 16)**

Published by Collins, An imprint of HarperCollins*Publishers*
77 – 85 Fulham Palace Road, Hammersmith, London, W6 8JB

Browse the complete Collins catalogue at
www.collinseducation.com

© HarperCollins*Publishers* Limited 2012
Previously published in 2007 by Folens
First published in 2003 by Belair Publications

10 9 8 7 6 5 4 3 2 1

ISBN-13 978-0-00-744796-1

Jean Evans asserts her moral rights to be identified as the author of this work

British Library Cataloguing in Publication Data
A Catalogue record for this publication is available from the British Library

All Early learning goals, Areas of learning and development, and Aspects of learning quoted in this book are taken from the *Statutory Framework for the Early Years Foundation Stage*, Department for Education, 2012 (available at www.education.gov.uk/publications). This information is licensed under the terms of the Open Government Licence (www.nationalarchives.gov.uk/doc/open-government-licence).

Every effort has been made to trace copyright holders and to obtain their permission for the use of copyright material. The authors and publishers will gladly receive any information enabling them to rectify any error or omission in subsequent editions.

Cover concept: Mount Deluxe              Cover design: Linda Miles, Lodestone Publishing
Cover photography: Nigel Meager       Commissioning editor: Zöe Nichols
Editor: Gaynor Spry                              Page layout: Suzanne Ward
Photography: Roger Brown, Marcus Pomfret and Kelvin Freeman

p19 Girl in reflective bib © Don Gray/Photofusion; p20 X-ray © CNRI/Science Photo Library

Printed and bound by Printing Express Limited, Hong Kong

MIX
Paper from
responsible sources
FSC™ C007454

# Contents

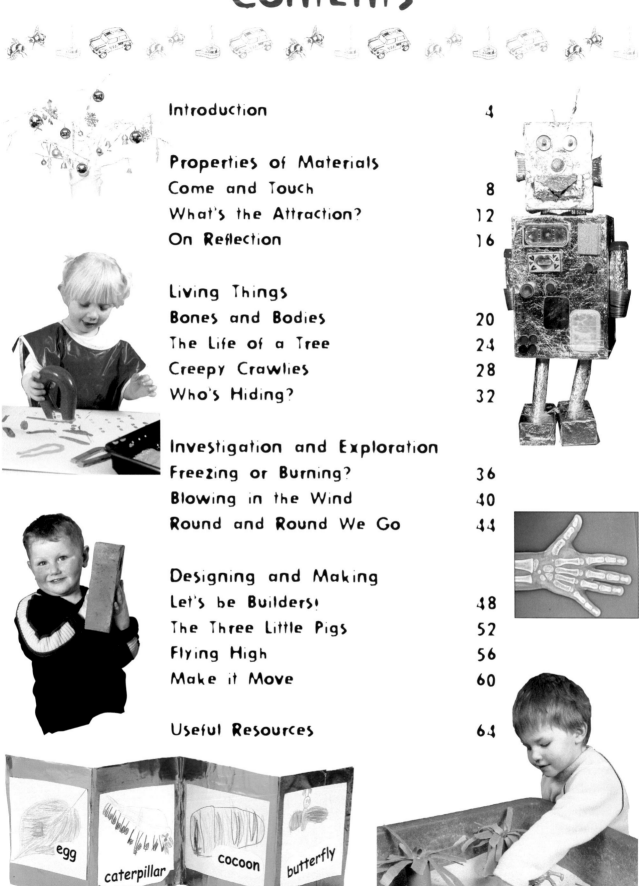

egg     caterpillar     cocoon     butterfly

# Introduction

The **Belair Early Years** series has been well-loved by early years educators working with the under-fives for many years. This re-launched edition of these practical resource books offers popular, tried and tested ideas, all written by professionals working in early years education. The inspirational ideas will support educators in delivering the three characteristics of effective teaching and learning identified in the Statutory Framework for the Early Years Foundation Stage 2012: playing and exploring, active learning, and creating and thinking critically.

The guiding principles at the heart of the EYFS Framework 2012 emphasise the importance of the unique child, the impact of positive relationships and enabling environments on children's learning and development, and that children develop and learn in different ways and at different rates. The 'hands on' activities in **Belair Early Years** fit this ethos perfectly and are ideal for developing the EYFS prime areas of learning (Communication and language, Physical development, Personal, social and emotional development) and specific areas of learning (Literacy, Mathematics, Understanding the world, Expressive arts and design) which should be implemented through a mix of child-initiated and adult-led activities. Purposeful play is vital for children's development, whether leading their own play or participating in play guided by adults. Where appropriate, suggestions for Free Play opportunities are identified.

Throughout this book full-colour photography is used to offer inspiration for presenting and developing children's individual work with creative display ideas for each theme. Display is highly beneficial as a stimulus for further exploration, as well as providing a visual communication of ideas and a creative record of children's learning journeys. In addition to descriptions of the activities, each theme in this book provides clear Learning Intentions and extension ideas and activities as Home Links to involve parents/carers in their child's learning.

This title, **Science**, particularly supports children's progress towards attaining the Early Learning Goals in the Understanding the world and Communication and language areas of learning. Children are naturally curious about the world in which they live, and practitioners can stimulate this curiosity further by providing new and exciting ways of observing and investigating. Learning associated vocabulary, and engaging in discussion, enhances children's ability to express to themselves clearly. These early investigations, and answering 'how' and 'why' questions about them, help children to understand the basics of scientific methodology.

When investigating and exploring, encourage children to:
- use all of their senses
- consider the properties of the materials they are exploring
- note and discuss similarities and differences
- talk about changes they observe
- use any new vocabulary they are introduced to in the appropriate context
- describe their ideas and conclusions clearly to others.

By following the above guidance, practitioners will help children to learn to:
- adopt a more sensory approach to explorations
- conduct their own investigations, particularly by extending initial exploration to find out more about an aspect that interests them
- reach conclusions based on observed features and reactions
- recognise that not all materials, or living things, behave in the same way
- understand more about living things and life processes
- describe their observations and communicate their ideas clearly to others.

Most significantly, they will begin to develop an awareness of scientific methods and a responsibility for controlling the direction and scope of own their learning.

I hope that adults and children alike will enjoy exploring the activities in this book.

Jean Evans

# The themes

The book is subdivided into four aspects of scientific discovery: Properties of Materials, Living Things, Investigation and Exploration, and Designing and Making. Ideas within each theme promote learning across the early years curriculum, such as Language and Literacy, Mathematics, Creative Work and Knowledge and Understanding of the World. Each theme includes specific Learning Intentions and helpful Starting Points.

A section on Free Play within each individual theme demonstrates how to provide valuable opportunities for children to learn through their own explorations and investigations. Also included are suggestions for Outdoor Activities, often neglected in overall planning, and an important area for scientific discovery.

Parents and carers play a significant part in a child's education. Home Links are provided in each theme, for extending ideas and activities into the home environment.

# Setting up the displays

- Take time to plan the display as a team, and remember to give consideration to the borders and table areas. Involve the children as often as possible from initial planning to final completion of the display.
- Create displays at child height whenever possible, so that the children can observe and touch them easily.

- Make sure that all titles, labels and captions are written clearly in simple lettering.
- Try to use different textures and create three-dimensional effects to encourage the children to touch the display and think about the content.
- Set up a table of resources linked to the wall display for children to explore freely.

# Science is everywhere

Scientific investigation can take place in all areas of the room, as well as outdoors. Children should be able to explore freely and make their own discoveries when they visit investigation areas, with and without adult support. Consideration should be given to the specific needs of individuals so that resources are easily accessible and adapted if necessary, for example, to support those with mobility problems.

# Setting up an investigation area

In addition to providing opportunities throughout the early years environment, it can be useful to set up investigation areas with a specific focus. This is especially important where there are safety issues, for example, working with sharp tools.

When setting up the area, try to enclose it on three sides if possible to give children a feeling of privacy and to encourage concentration. Attach appropriate pictures, posters and photographs to screens and walls, and stand reference books close by, to stimulate children's thinking and extend their knowledge. Supply a good, safe working area, such as a strong table or workbench at child height. Make sure resources are easily accessible and have a designated place for storage.

Always include writing tools and materials so that children can record the results of their observations.

# Storage of equipment

It is important when setting up a storage system in an investigation area to make all items easily accessible to the children. They should be able to find what they want and know exactly where to put that item after they have finished. Screens with shelves can be used to store some items, for example, tools such as screwdrivers and files. Create shadows of the items from sticky-backed plastic and attach these to the shelves. Larger items, such as ladles, whisks and sieves, can be hung by loops of string onto plastic hooks on the backs of screens next to their shadows. Smaller resources, such as nails or conkers, can be stored in plastic containers. Label all containers clearly to indicate the contents, and arrange them on a table or shelf.

For those who have a limited amount of space, consider using trolleys to store equipment and bring these out for each session. Use shadows and hooks as described above, and store small tools and equipment in labelled plastic boxes with removable lids. Trolleys can also be useful for outdoor investigation.

# Working safely

- Always check for allergies and dietary restrictions when planning activities and resourcing investigative areas.
- Floors can get messy and cause accidents so include equipment for children to sweep up and dispose of rubbish when they have finished in the area.
- Indicate clearly how many children can work in the area at any one time, for example, by putting up a sign or only having the correct number of aprons available.
- Supply safety aprons and eye protection if appropriate, and make sure children know how to use them.
- Emphasise safe use of equipment by modelling this to children when they first enter a newly set up area.
- Hang up a list of safety rules so that all adults can reinforce these with the children who work there.
- Never use glass containers.

# Come and Touch

## Learning Intentions

- To show curiosity and interest in things around them.

- To investigate natural objects and man-made materials through the sense of sight and touch.

## Starting Points

- Pass around a 'feely' box full of small objects with contrasting textures, such as a smooth cotton reel, a spiky pine cone and a rough piece of sandpaper. Invite each child to put a hand in the box and choose an object to describe to the rest of the group using the sense of touch. Ask the children to guess what is being described and then reveal the object.

## Display

- Back a low display board in light-coloured paper. Divide the board into three sections. Make a border for the display by sticking recycled natural and man-made materials onto strips of paper. Use materials with varying textures.

- Talk to the children about the different materials and create appropriate captions for each section, such as 'Rough or smooth?'

- Invite the children to arrange samples of different surfaces on the backing paper and glue them on. Use staples as well if necessary, but do not let the children handle the staple gun.

# Language and Literacy

- Encourage the children to think of different words to describe how an object feels, for example, describing a teddy as 'soft', 'tickly', 'fluffy', 'cuddly' and 'warm'.

- Make 'feely' books. Stick scraps of different materials to pieces of card and fasten them together by punching holes in the card and tying thick wool through them. Include the children's words to describe the textures on each page.

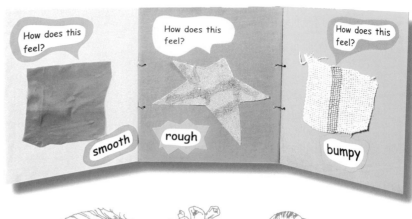

# Free Play

- Put natural materials, such as twigs, shells and small stones, into wet and dry sand trays so that children can use them for imaginary play.

- Use natural materials in role-play, for example, as produce in shops or food in cafés.

- Include a selection of natural and man-made materials in the water tray so that children can investigate whether they will float or sink.

# Mathematics

- Put two hoops on a carpet and invite the children to sort a basket of items into two categories, for example, rough and smooth, hard and soft, wood and metal, rigid and flexible.

- Create collage patterns by gluing natural materials to sheets of card.

- Play a 'texture' number game. Stick five tiny samples of natural and man-made materials to long strips of card numbered one to five. Create smaller matching cards to fit over each section. The object of the game is to cover all five of the materials on the large card with smaller matching cards.

# Creative Work

- Supply rigid and flexible materials in separate containers for children to use freely in model-making and construction work.

- Glue a short length of string to a block of wood in a random shape and allow to dry. Dip the block in paint to print repeat patterns.

# Our World

- Make a collection of different materials for a 'feely' table. Include small bags with a texture attached to the front. Ask the children to put objects with a similar surface into each bag.

- Change the objects on the 'feely' table daily to give new experiences.

- Alternatively, organise two tables under the display. Cover one in a natural-coloured fabric and display a selection of natural materials to feel and explore, such as shells, seeds, pieces of wood and small containers of sand. Cover the other in a contrasting, brightly-coloured fabric and display a selection of rigid and flexible items on it, such as ribbon, flexible plastic tubing and a spoon.

- Encourage the children to talk about how the objects look and feel. Include magnifying glasses so that they can examine them more closely.

# Outdoor Activities

- Go for walks to collect natural materials and examine them on return to the classroom.

- Provide opportunities for children to handle soil and compost in outdoor containers, for example, as they plant seeds and bulbs.

- Make rubbings of different surfaces, such as bark, fencing, walls and paths.

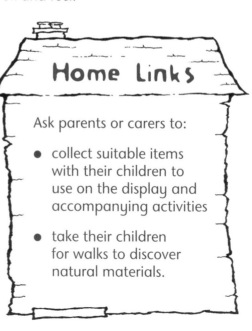

## Home Links

Ask parents or carers to:

- collect suitable items with their children to use on the display and accompanying activities

- take their children for walks to discover natural materials.

# What's the Attraction?

## Starting Points

- Encourage children to explore different types of magnets, including fridge magnets, and make a collection of magnetic and non-magnetic materials.

## Display

- Make a large tree by cutting out textured paper, such as blown vinyl wallpaper, and stapling it to a board in folds to form a trunk and branches. Paint the tree and then stick on green tissue leaves.

- Make some magnetic apples for the tree using circles of red card with a small magnet attached to the back of each. Glue the other half of the magnet to the tree.

- Invite the children to 'stick' their apples to the tree. Talk about how the magnet enables the apple to stay on the tree.

- Set out a table in front of the display with a selection of magnets, magnetic and non-magnetic materials, so that the children can explore them freely. Include books about magnets. Provide clipboards, with pencils attached, so that children can 'record' the results of their observations.

# Language and Literacy

- Divide a group of objects into those that attract magnets and those that do not. Make a label for each object and invite the children to place the labels alongside the correct objects. Talk about initial letter sounds. Regroup the objects into those that start with the same letter.

- Invite the children to paint or draw pictures of magnets, and things that are attracted to them, and make a 'Magnet' book. Help them to write appropriate labels and captions.

# Free Play

- Organise a 'magnet' box containing the resources used as a starting point and store this where children can access it freely.

- Attach paperclips to small cars and invite children to try pulling them along with magnets.

# Mathematics

- Sit in a group and ask a child to draw a tree on the whiteboard. Attach a few apples from the display to the board and give the children number challenges based on the apples. Ask, for example, 'How many apples are on the tree?', 'One fell off, how many now?' Use glove puppets of woodland creatures (who come and remove an apple) to make the counting more fun.

- Make up a rhyme about 'Ten green apples hanging on a tree', based on the rhyme 'Ten green bottles'. Put ten apple magnets on the display and remove one as each verse is sung.

# Creative Work

- Put some iron filings in a clear, shallow container with a lid and move a magnet slowly underneath to create patterns.

- Use horseshoe, circular and rod-shaped magnets dipped in paint to print shapes and patterns.

# Our World

- Invite children to play with engines and trucks that join together with magnets. Draw their attention to the function of the magnets. What happens if a truck is turned round? Introduce the words 'attract' and 'repel'.

# Outdoor Activities

- Provide a box of larger magnets outdoors so that children can investigate whether different surfaces are magnetic.

- Make salt dough magnet apples using equal quantities of salt and self-raising flour, mixed to a stiff dough with water.

- Create flat apple shapes with the dough and push a small magnet into the back of each one.

- Take the magnets back out and bake the apples in a slow oven until hard.

- Ask the children to glue the magnets back into the holes in the apples. Supply appropriate paint colours so that the children can paint the apples, leave them to dry and then coat them with a PVA glue varnish.

- Place in a box and use a large magnet to collect the apples.

## Home Links

Ask parents or carers to:

- help their children to look for items that use magnets around the home, for example, fridge magnets and door catches.

# On Reflection

## Learning Intentions

- To become aware of similarities and differences in materials.

- To discover some of the uses of reflective materials.

## Starting Points

- Invite the children to look at their reflections in a mirror. Introduce the word 'reflection'. Can the children think of any other things that they can see reflections in, such as spoons, foil or still water?

- Suggest making a display of reflective materials.

## Display

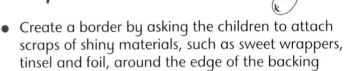

- Create a border by asking the children to attach scraps of shiny materials, such as sweet wrappers, tinsel and foil, around the edge of the backing paper.

- Cut out a large star from card and supply the children with lots of recycled shiny materials to glue to the surface of it. Attach the star to the centre of the display. Surround the star with individual collage pictures the children have made from the shiny material scraps.

- Choose an appropriate title for the display and cut out letters from shiny paper to make the words. Glue them along the top of the display. Attach other reflective objects, such as CDs, foil curls, tinsel and stars. Attach any three-dimensional work, such as shiny robots, to the display.

# Language and Literacy

- Wrap a small box in hologram paper or use a hologram gift bag. Play 'Pass the parcel', and when the music stops invite the child holding the bag to think of a word to describe it, such as 'shiny', 'glittery', 'smooth', 'hard'. Print out the words and mount them on black card. Attach the bag to the wall alongside the display, with the words around it.

- Use the same bag or box and encourage the children to pretend that there is an animal inside it. When the music stops, invite the child holding the parcel to make appropriate animal noises as a clue to help the other children to guess the imaginary contents.

- Invite the children to create greetings cards for special birthdays and festivals using glitter, sequins, coloured foil and shiny paper. Encourage them to write their names and attempt additional words if they are able.

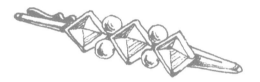

bright

smooth

sparkles

shiny

glittery

## Free Play

- Stand a table in front of the display, covered in shiny material. Use it to arrange shiny objects and reflective materials for the children to explore.

# Mathematics

- Create robots by gluing boxes together and covering them with foil and other shiny materials. Talk about the size and shape of the boxes, and make comparisons between the heights of the robots.

- Cut out cellophane shapes and attach them to windows. Invite the children to look through them and ask them questions to encourage observation, for example, 'What can you see through the blue triangle? Does anything look different?'

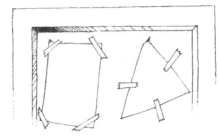

# Creative Work

- Create jewellery from shiny materials. Cut out card crowns and attach shiny collage materials, and make necklaces and bracelets from string with sweet wrappers and foil threaded along it.

- Leave a safety mirror on a table along with some shiny jewellery and hair ornaments so that children can have fun changing their appearances.

- Invite the children to move freely to dreamy music, pretending to be stars floating around the sky, or pieces of foil twisting in the breeze.

- Ask the children to watch as you scrunch up a piece of cellophane and then let it spring slowly back into position. Invite them to pretend to be cellophane, curling up tightly and then jerking back into a flat position.

# Our World

- Talk about how reflective materials are used to keep people safe, for example, shiny strips worn at night, orange tabards and bicycle reflectors.

- Make 'magic glasses' by using card with coloured cellophane over the front of each eyepiece. Invite children to look through the cellophane and to talk about how the world has changed. Encourage them to say whether they like or dislike the effect of changing the colours of familiar objects.

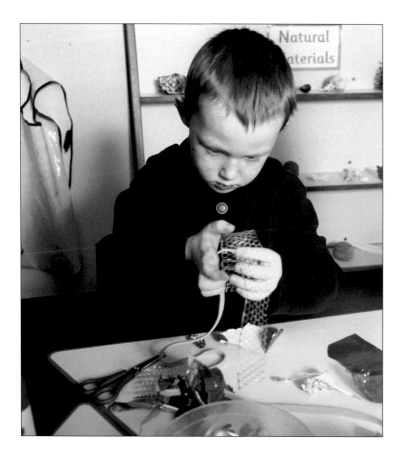

- Make a shiny hanging. Thread foil strips, old CDs and other reflective materials onto a thick lace and hang from a tree branch outside. Observe how the sunlight is reflected as it moves. Talk about the colours the children can see and make comparisons with rainbows. Hang non-reflective items alongside it, such as wooden spoons and cardboard tubes, and make comparisons.

# Outdoor Activities

- Look for reflections in bowls of water or puddles on a sunny day. What happens to the reflection when the water is swirled around or the puddles are stamped on?

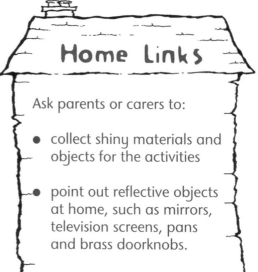

## Home Links

Ask parents or carers to:

- collect shiny materials and objects for the activities

- point out reflective objects at home, such as mirrors, television screens, pans and brass doorknobs.

# Bones and Bodies

## Learning Intentions

- To use appropriate vocabulary to describe the main parts of the body.

- To learn about the function of bones.

## Starting points

- Read *Funnybones* by Janet and Allan Ahlberg (Picture Puffins).

- Sing 'Head and shoulders, knees and toes' and add appropriate actions.

- Talk about the children's experience and knowledge of bones. Have they ever broken a bone and visited hospital? Look at an X-ray.

## Display

- Draw around three children and cut out the outlines. Paint one outline black and the other two outlines in skin tones. Back a large wall with brightly-coloured paper and divide it into three sections. Create borders from hand and footprints to separate the three sections.

- Use a poster or book to remind the children about the bones inside us.

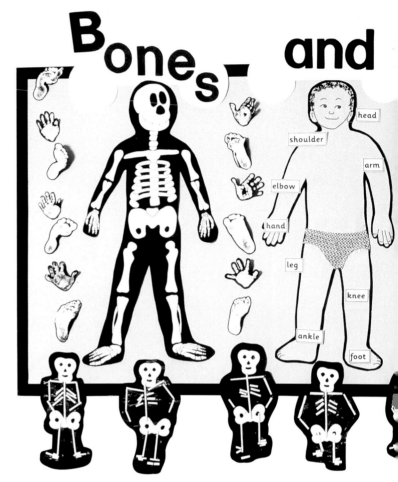

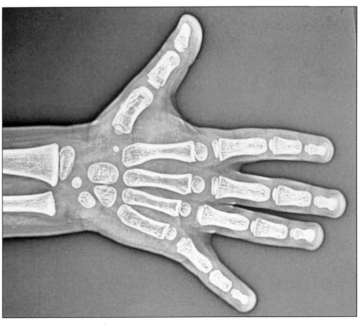

- Invite the children to glue paper bones onto the black outline in the appropriate places, using the book to help with positioning. Add hair and facial features to the other two outlines using collage materials. Attach underwear to one and dress the other in clothes.

- Attach the outlines to the wall and add appropriate labels to each outline, naming the basic bones and the body parts.

- Under the display, arrange the children's model bones, books and puzzles about body parts and a small model skeleton.

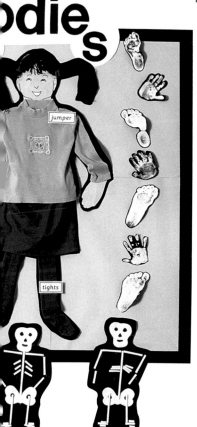

## Language and Literacy

- Talk about the supporting function of the skeleton. What would happen if we had no bones? Compare our bodies with creatures without bones, such as worms. Can the children wriggle like a worm?

- Ask the children to take off their shoes and discover what feet can do. Can they pick up a pencil with their feet? Now try with a hand. Which is easier? Can the children say why?

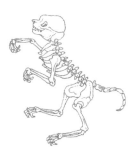

## Free Play

- Have a collection of sterilised real bones (animal skulls, teeth) for the children to touch and investigate with magnifying glasses, tweezers and tongs.

- Bury real bones or model bones previously made by the children in the sandpit. Add spoons and encourage the children to dig for 'dinosaur' bones.

- Turn the role-play area into a hospital. Add bandages, doctor's kit, uniforms, posters showing the bones, and X-ray pictures.

# Mathematics

- Ask the children to count how many fingers they have on each hand and how many thumbs. How many digits altogether? Feel and count the bones in a finger and a thumb. Are they the same?

- Find the 'longest' and 'shortest' finger and toe.

- Create hand and footprints with a group of children and arrange them in order of size.

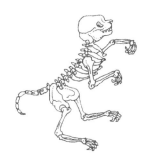

# Creative Work

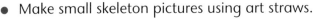

- Display a poster showing the bones in the body near the painting table. Provide black paper and white chalk and encourage the children to draw their own skeletons.

- Make small skeleton pictures using art straws.

- Experiment with cutting sponge. Dip the sponge shapes into white paint and print a bone design on black paper or fabric.

- Make model bones and skeletons from clay and paint them white.

22

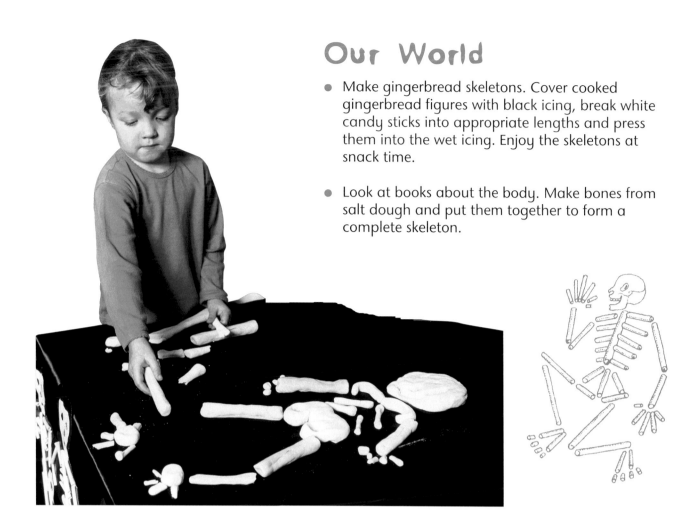

## Our World

- Make gingerbread skeletons. Cover cooked gingerbread figures with black icing, break white candy sticks into appropriate lengths and press them into the wet icing. Enjoy the skeletons at snack time.

- Look at books about the body. Make bones from salt dough and put them together to form a complete skeleton.

## Outdoor Activities

- Supply children with chalk to draw around each other on a dry surface and encourage them to draw their bones within the outline.

- Make a list of physical actions the children can do, such as run, jump, hop and skip. Talk about the parts of the body involved in each movement. Draw a picture of each action on a large card and write the name of the action underneath. Mix all of the cards up and choose a child to pick out a card and hold it up. Follow the action on the card and stop at a chosen signal, such as a ringing bell. Choose a different card and continue.

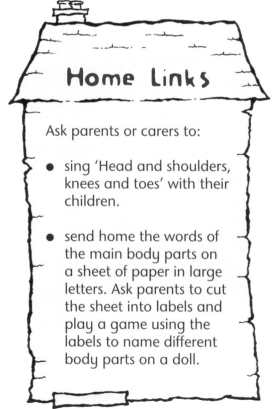

### Home Links

Ask parents or carers to:

- sing 'Head and shoulders, knees and toes' with their children.

- send home the words of the main body parts on a sheet of paper in large letters. Ask parents to cut the sheet into labels and play a game using the labels to name different body parts on a doll.

# The Life of a Tree

## Learning Intentions

- To discover and name the different parts of a tree.

- To explore what is needed to sustain the life of a tree.

## Starting Points

- Go for a walk to look at trees. Touch the trunk and talk about what it feels like. Collect some samples of leaves and bark to observe more closely indoors, as well as seeds or fruits according to the season.

- Set up a 'growing table' with carrot tops, mustard and cress seeds and small plants.

## Display

- Cut out a large outline of a tree. Invite the children to feel a piece of bark and suggest that they try to recreate the texture by sticking strips of crumpled newspaper to the tree outline and painting it brown.

- Attach the tree to the centre of the wall, leaving space for children's work at either side. Look at books and photographs of trees throughout the year and talk about seasonal changes. Add leaves, blossom, seeds or fruits to the tree according to the season, created from collage materials, rubbings or printing with leaves.

- Display children's paintings of trees and collage work around the tree.

# Language and Literacy

- Look at books, gardening catalogues and pictures and talk about the conditions needed for seeds to grow.

- Name the different parts of a tree, such as trunk, leaves, buds, seeds, fruits, blossom and roots.

- Dramatise the story of 'Jack and the Beanstalk'.

## Free Play

- Include tree-related items such as twigs, cones, acorns, conkers and leaves in sand and water trays so that children can explore their properties.

- Set up an interest table of objects made from wood.

- Encourage children to work with wood by supplying a woodwork bench, a selection of wood offcuts, a vice and simple tools such as sanding blocks, saws and files.

 **Note**: Always supervise the use of woodwork tools.

# Mathematics

- Walk in a park or woodland and point to the tallest and shortest tree. Estimate which is the fattest tree and check by measuring the girth with a length of string or long strip of paper.

- Sort a box of leaves according to size, shape or colour. Use appropriate mathematical language as you do so, for example, 'pointed', 'round', 'widest', 'narrowest', 'smaller than' and 'bigger than'.

- Mount a variety of different leaves on card and cover with sticky-backed plastic. Use to play matching games such as 'snap' and 'lotto'.

- Plant sunflower seeds and measure their growth. Make comparisons between the tallest and shortest.

# Creative Work

- Create collage pictures from a selection of seeds.

- Invite the children to curl up tightly and pretend to be seeds. Suggest that they open up as the seed germinates and gradually stretch upwards towards the light until they become tall trees waving their branches in the wind.

# Our World

- Talk about the seasons and make a seasonal branch. Include bare branches sparkling with glitter 'frost' in winter, pink and white crumpled tissue 'blossom' and tiny green crepe paper leaves in spring, large leaves made from fabric scraps in summer and brightly-painted leaves and appropriate fruits as the leaves begin to fall.

- Talk about the living things that live or shelter in a tree, such as birds, insects, squirrels and bats. Set up a 'hollow tree' role-play area using large packing cases draped in brown fabric so that children can pretend to be these creatures.

- Plant conkers or other seeds from trees in pots or directly into the ground and observe their growth.

# Outdoor Activities

- Plant potatoes in the ground or in buckets and observe how the young potatoes grow on the roots of the plant.

- Fill a parachute with dry leaves and have fun lifting it up and watching the leaves float back down again through the air.

## Home Links

- Send home sunflower seedlings the children have planted, with instructions for their care.

Ask parents or carers to:

- help their children to hunt for things made of wood, both indoors and outdoors.

# Creepy Crawlies

## Learning Intentions

- To discover similarities and differences between minibeasts.

- To explore change by learning about life cycles.

## Starting Points

- Talk about the children's experiences of minibeasts. How many can they name? Where might they find these creatures?

- Look at books and pictures of minibeasts and compare their features.

## Display

- Back the display in appropriate colours to depict a natural habitat. Invite the children to create plants and stones using shredded paper or crumpled tissue balls.

- Ask the children to think of minibeasts that might live in their picture, looking at books to give them further ideas. Use a variety of collage materials to make ladybirds, snails, woodlice, butterflies, worms, spiders and ants. Create spiders' webs from silver thread or grey wool and stretch these across the bushes. Add the minibeasts the children have made, in appropriate positions.

# Language and Literacy

- Invite the children to create zigzag books about the life cycle of a minibeast. Fold a long strip of card to form the pages and ask the children to draw a different stage in the life cycle on each page. Help them to label the different stages.

- Look closely at some snails and talk about the spiral shape of the shells. Invite the children to draw spiral snail shells or follow spiral lines with a pencil. Talk about the movements of worms and draw some wiggly lines. Make comparisons between spiral, straight and curved lines.

# Free Play

- Leave some plastic minibeasts in the construction area. Encourage the children to take turns to hide one of them and give positional clues to the others to help them to find it, for example, 'Look behind the red brick.'

- Cook some spaghetti in water with added red food colouring. Put the cooled pink 'worms' into some water and invite the children to explore the texture.

- Add laminated child-made minibeasts to the sand tray along with some pretend or real dried leaves. Encourage the children to play freely, creating imaginary homes for the creatures.

# Mathematics

- Make a large minibeast with detachable legs (use Velcro). Use the minibeast for simple counting problems in addition and subtraction.

- Invite the children to make some clay worms and arrange them in a row according to length.

- Ask the children to sponge-print circles of red, black and green and transform them into ladybirds, spiders and frogs by drawing the appropriate number of legs with felt-tip pens.

- Suggest that the children add small, black, sticky spots to ladybird prints, making sure that both sides have the same number of dots.

# Creative  Work

- Make mobiles representing the life cycle of a butterfly.

- Re-enact the rhyme 'Incy Wincy spider' using spiders made from balls of scrunched up tissue with pipe cleaner legs. Tie the spiders to black thread and pull them through plastic drainpipes.

# Our World

- Follow the instructions on a packet of green jelly. Ask the children to watch from a safe distance when adding the hot water. Pour the dissolved mixture into a shallow bowl. Add some jelly worms and drop in some currants to represent frogs' eggs. Enjoy eating the 'minibeasts pond' at snack time.

- Make a collection of books about minibeasts and display them on a table with plastic minibeasts, a real wormery and magnifying glasses.

# Outdoor Activities

- Go on a 'bug hunt'. Ensure that there will be creatures to find by putting stones and logs in the area beforehand. Supply the children with plastic containers to store their catch so that they can bring them indoors to observe more closely before returning them to their habitat.

## Home Links

Ask parents or carers to:

- help their children to find minibeasts under stones and wood in gardens and during country walks

- help the children to keep a tally of the creatures they find on a sample chart.

# Who's Hiding?

Who's hiding?

## Learning Intentions

- To develop observational skills.

- To make comparisons between the features of different jungle creatures.

## Starting Points

- Visit a library with a group to choose a selection of books about jungle animals. Display them in the book area to stimulate interest.

- Cover a shoe box with pictures of jungle animals cut from a sheet of wrapping paper. Laminate some jungle animal pictures and attach hanging loops to the back. Put them in the box.

## Display

- Create tree branches from strips of twisted newspaper. Staple the branches loosely across a green background and paint them brown. Create a pool from crumpled foil or blue cellophane.

- Look at books about jungle creatures and make these animals using collage and painting materials. Attach them to the wall, tucking them behind the branches.

- Screw cup hooks into the display, just below each animal or bird.

- Create creepers from lengths of thin rope dipped in green paint with tissue leaves glued along them. Drape the creepers around the edge and across the front of the display to create an impression of rich vegetation.

- Place the jungle box below the display so that the children can hang the animals on the wall hooks beside the appropriate creatures. Add a selection of appropriate 'small world' animals and books about jungle life.

# Language and Literacy

- Stimulate children's interest during group discussions by creating a jungle pool from a small circle of stones and asking them to sit around it. Place a working table water feature in the centre of the stones and arrange model frogs and insects around it. Change the creatures daily to encourage imaginative talk.

- Enclose the book corner in drapes of green and blue fabric to create a comfortable 'secret garden' for quiet reading.

# Free Play

- Create a model jungle by putting compost into a sand tray. Include twigs, string and tissue to create vegetation and appropriate 'small world' animals to play with.

# Mathematics

- Discuss the position of the animals on the display using appropriate positional language such as 'behind the creeper' and 'under the water'.

- Sort 'small world' animals according to their patterns, for example, stripes or spots.

# Creative Work

- Talk about woodland creatures that hide. Invite the children to create masks from card, wool and fabric scraps, and supply lengths of coloured fabric so that they can dress up as these creatures.

- Create a woodland den in which the children can play, wearing the masks.

- Organise a role-play trek into the jungle. Discuss what you will need to take, for example, sun protection, as well as cameras and binoculars to observe and record jungle life. Invite each child to pack a bag and travel around the room imagining what they might see.

- Use large and small apparatus to create a jungle obstacle course for children to negotiate, for example, using carpet tiles as stepping-stones, benches as fallen logs and tunnels as thick undergrowth.

# Our World

- Use large sheets of coloured card to represent water, farm land, countryside and jungle and invite the children to sort a selection of 'small world' animals into groups according to where they live, for example, land and water, or wild and domesticated.

- Create caves from large apparatus draped in old curtains so that children can pretend to be wild animals.

# Outdoor Activities

- Find out about creatures that hide in a swamp. Create a swamp outside in a trough. Add coloured water, strips of cellophane and tissue paper, stones and leaves. Hide plastic swamp animals for the children to find.

This is the 'Hollow Tree Log' Two children Only Please

Please Keep Our Woodland Tidy!

## Home Links

Ask parents or carers to:

- help their children pack a rucksack and go for a trek in some woods, imagining that they are jungle explorers

- take their child to a zoo or safari park to observe wild animals.

35

# Freezing or Burning?

## Learning Intentions

- To make comparisons between hot and cold.

- To discover the dangers of fire.

## Starting Points

- Pass around clothes that would be worn on very hot and very cold days, and discuss with the children their experiences of weather conditions. Then make comparisons between things that are hot and cold.

- Invite a fire crew to visit to talk to the children about the dangers of fire and to show them some of the resources used to fight fires.

- Look at books and pictures about animals that live in cold lands.

## Display

- Divide the display space into two. Back one side in a 'warm' colour, such as red or orange, and the other in a 'cold' colour, such as blue or white. Create a border of foil or white corrugated paper icicles around the 'cold' section and create a paper border of flames around the other.

- Make a large fire from collage materials in the centre of the 'hot' section using twigs, crepe paper, cellophane and tissue.

- Paint or sponge-print 'fire' pictures with red, yellow and orange paint.

- Create 'frosty pictures' using white paint, silver glitter, foil and shiny paper, cellophane, tissue and crepe paper in 'cold' colours.

- Ask the children to think of 'hot' and 'cold' words, such as 'sizzle', 'burn', 'freeze' and 'ice', and add these to the display.

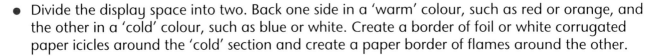

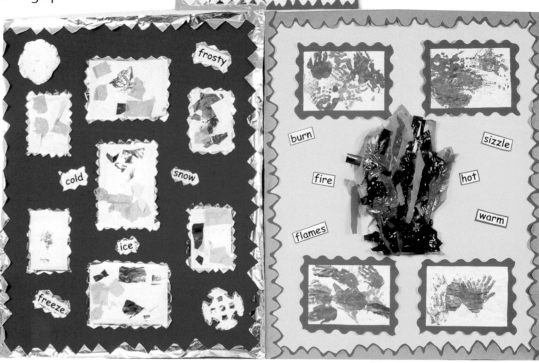

# Language and Literacy

- Make a set of word cards for the children to match to the words on the display.

- Ask the children to make summer and winter books by cutting out pictures from catalogues, magazines and travel brochures and sticking them to sheets of paper.

# Free Play

- Add ice (or if possible snow) to the water tray and plastic animals, such as polar bears and penguins. Alternatively, provide scoops and spades in the water tray for the children to investigate the properties of the ice. How quickly does it melt?

- In contrast, create a desert in the sand tray with plastic camels, a foil dish oasis and cardboard tube palm trees.

# Mathematics

- Sort clothes into two suitcases, for holidays in a cold or a hot country.

- Look closely at snowflakes under a magnifying glass and talk about the patterns. If there is no snow available look at a picture of a snowflake. Invite the children to make snowflakes of their own by folding circles of white paper into quarters and then cutting out small pieces along the folded edges before opening the circles out again.

# Creative Work

- Create a 'small world' cold land by taping screwed up pieces of newspaper over the surface of a table and draping it with a white sheet. Add a foil pool and appropriate plastic animals and people.

- Make igloos for 'small world' people from upturned plastic yoghurt pots covered in bubble wrap, white tissue and white fabric scraps sprinkled with glitter.

- Make polar bears from white modelling clay or salt dough painted white.

- Create penguins from yoghurt pots covered in fabric, with shiny paper features.

- Make seals from old white or grey socks. Snip off the toe and stuff this with soft material. Fasten the end with an elastic band to create the tail. Stick on two felt eyes.

# Our World

- Extend the children's knowledge and understanding of their own and other cultures by linking the theme to Autumn and Winter festivals associated with fire or light, such as Bonfire Night, Diwali or Hanukkah, for example, by creating bonfire collage pictures, diva lamps from clay or a Menorah from cardboard tubes.

- Leave water outside overnight in shallow containers on very cold days to create ice or make some in the freezer. Melt the ice using salt, warm water or direct sunlight and talk about what happens.

- On winter days, explore the properties of snow. Provide buckets, shovels, jugs and magnifying glasses for free investigation.

# Outdoor Activities

- Encourage the children to take part in vigorous exercise, such as running, hopping and skipping. Talk about feeling hot after exercise and cooling down again.

- Take the children outdoors on a cold day dressed in thick coats, hats, gloves and scarves, or on a hot day wearing T-shirts and shorts. Talk about the right clothes needed for certain weather. What would happen if we wore summer clothes in the winter and vice versa?

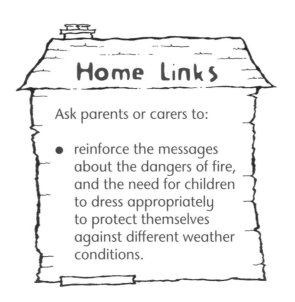

## Home Links

Ask parents or carers to:

- reinforce the messages about the dangers of fire, and the need for children to dress appropriately to protect themselves against different weather conditions.

# Blowing in the Wind

## Learning Intentions

- To learn more about the properties of air.

- To discover how things work and why things happen.

## Starting Points

- Invite the children to run outdoors on a windy day and talk about how the wind feels against their faces. Discuss things that fly in the wind, including living things such as birds and seeds, and man-made objects such as gliders and parachutes.

## Display

- Back the display space in blue paper to represent the sky and add clouds made from white tissue, fabric or wool.

- Create a border by attaching children's bubble prints to the edge of the blue paper.

- Talk about things that move in the wind, and suggest that the children make some of these items. Supply them with a wide range of suitable collage materials to support and develop their ideas.

- Make windmills from squares of brightly-coloured paper. Cut a line diagonally halfway into the centre of the square from each corner. Fold a point from each corner into the centre and push a sharp tool through the four points. Push a plastic straw with a 'bendy' neck through the hole created so that the windmill can spin. Tape over the end of the straw at the front and bend the straw to form a handle.

- Create fans by folding sheets of paper in a zigzag pattern. Tape one end together, tightly folded, and leave the other end to open out into a fan shape.

- Make flags from rectangles of fabric taped to short lengths of dowelling.

- Secure the finished models onto the 'sky' background.

# Language and Literacy

- Create a role-play hot-air balloon or glider from large boxes and encourage children to imagine journeys to fantastic places.

- Ask the children to lie on their backs, close their eyes and pretend to be floating in the air in a glider, parachute or hot-air balloon. Collect words such as 'float', 'glide' and 'drift' to describe the sensation. Print the words and add them to the display.

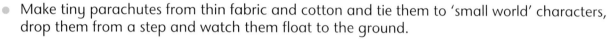

# Free Play

- Make tiny parachutes from thin fabric and cotton and tie them to 'small world' characters, drop them from a step and watch them float to the ground.

# Mathematics

- Look at designs on flags from countries around the world and suggest that the children design their own repeat patterns on paper fans and flags.

- Extend children's awareness of shape by making simple kites using two pieces of thin dowelling taped together to form a cross. Glue the cross to a sheet of tissue paper and cut out a diamond shape. Decorate the kites by sponge-printing circles, squares and triangles onto the tissue. Create tails for the kites and add tissue-paper bows.

# Creative Work

- Make bubble prints by pouring a small amount of watery paint into a plastic pot and adding a squeeze of washing-up liquid. Ask the children to blow through straws into the liquid until the bubbles rise over the top of the pot. Demonstrate how to press a piece of paper over the bubbles to take a print.

- Talk about living things that fly, such as bees, butterflies and birds, and create mobiles of these from recycled materials.

# Our World

- Talk about the purpose of weather vanes and make a windsock from a tube of thin fabric tied with string to a fence post. Together, observe changes in wind direction.

- Create a wind chime by hanging metal objects, such as keys, cans, spoons and small bells, to a metal coat hanger. Suspend your chime from a branch or washing line and invite the children to talk about what they can hear.

# Outdoor Activities

- Play group games with a large, coloured parachute.

- Encourage the children to observe the effect of the wind by dancing with streamers, waving their flags and fans, and running with their kites and windmills.

- Create gliders by taping or gluing together two pieces of balsa wood. Which designs are the most successful when the children run and launch them into the air?

## Home Links

- Send home instructions for making a simple kite and encourage parents to fly kites with their children.

Listen to our metal mobile

# Round and Round We Go

## Learning Intentions

- To explore the function of wheels.

- To observe and create patterns.

## Starting Points

- Take the children for a walk to look for wheels in the environment. Discuss their size, shape and function.

- Look for wheels indoors and outdoors, for example, on bikes, trolleys, pedal cars, dolls' buggies and 'small world' vehicles.

## Display

- Create a background by taping together lengths of brightly-coloured strong paper, slightly bigger than the space available. Spread this on a large sheet of plastic, on top of a dry, flat, hard surface.

- Lay a rectangle of thick sponge on top of the plastic, alongside the paper, so that the children can ride straight over the sponge and onto the paper. The rectangle must be wider than the width of the largest vehicle and long enough for the circumference of the biggest tyre to pass across it. Soak the sponge in thick, dark-coloured paint.

- Invite the children to choose a vehicle and demonstrate how to position it at one end of the sponge rectangle so that they can ride in a straight line over it and onto the paper. (Make sure the children are well-protected in overalls or cut-down shirts.)

- What happens when they ride over the paper? Explain that the paint on the tyres has made prints or tracks. (Wipe the tyres clean after use.)

- Once the paper has been covered with tyre prints hang it on the display space and trim the edges to fit. Create a border by running 'small world' vehicles through a tray of paint and along strips of paper.

- Attach a selection of small and large wheels, cogs and construction kit wheels to the display over the prints.

- Under the display, have a small tray of dry sand and a selection of sand wheels and scoops for the children to explore.

# Language and Literacy

- Sing action rhymes associated with circular movements, such as 'The wheels on the bus', 'Wind the bobbin up' and 'Round and round the garden'. Encourage the children to listen for rhyming words and to make up their own verses.

- Develop handwriting skills by encouraging the children to draw circles in the air, both clockwise and anticlockwise. Supply different materials for them to draw circles, both indoors and outdoors, for example, using twigs in soil, chalk on the ground and crayons on paper.

# Free Play

- Supply the children with a range of recycled materials to create their own models of wheeled vehicles. Include circular items, such as foil dishes, paper plates and plastic lids.

- Include water wheels in the sand tray, whisks in the water tray, drills at the woodwork bench, pastry wheels on the dough table and paint rollers in the creative area to encourage children to explore the function of wheels through play.

# Mathematics

- Talk about the patterns made by the small vehicles as they are pushed through wet sand, over dough, through paint or in and out of water.

- Count the number of wheels on small and large vehicles. Which vehicle has the most? How many wheels have two cars? or three cars?

Printing with cars

# Creative Work

- Dip 'small world' cars and trains into paint and roll along a thin strip of paper, such as a till roll. Attach the finished prints to a door surround or window frame.

- Place a circular piece of paper in the bottom of a salad spinner. Drop different-coloured, watery paint gently onto it with a paintbrush. Put the lid on the salad spinner and turn several times to create a colourful pattern on the paper.

# Our World

- Show the children a picture of someone riding a unicycle and talk about the need to balance carefully when riding unicycles or bicycles. Do the children have stabilisers on their bicycles?

- Make models using construction equipment with cogs and gears. Look inside a clock and explain how the mechanism moves.

- Invite someone with an interesting vehicle, such as a tractor, milk float, mobile library or vintage car, to visit and talk about it.

# Outdoor Activities

- Supply cloths and buckets of water so that the children can wash the wheeled toys. Encourage them to ride around making prints with the wet tyres.

- Go for a walk to look for tracks, such as animal prints, footprints and tyre marks in mud or snow.

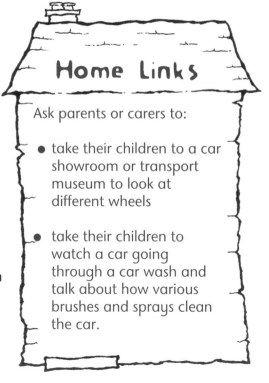

## Home Links

Ask parents or carers to:

- take their children to a car showroom or transport museum to look at different wheels

- take their children to watch a car going through a car wash and talk about how various brushes and sprays clean the car.

# Let's Be Builders!

## Learning Intentions

- To discover more about the materials needed to construct a house.

- To extend vocabulary to include words associated with building and construction.

## Starting Points

- Take the children outdoors to look at buildings. Invite them to touch a variety of surfaces, such as walls, door handles, fencing and guttering.

- Take a photograph of a house and some close-up shots of the different structural parts, such as the wall, roof, window and door. Use the photographs to stimulate discussions about houses.

## Display

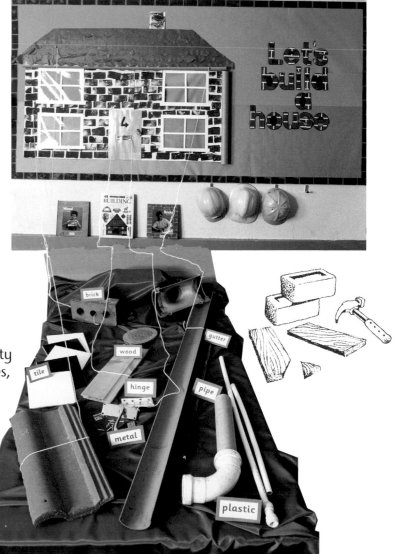

- Create a large house on the display board using collage materials, for example, wood-effect wallpaper for doors and window frames, cellophane for windowpanes and red, textured wallpaper for bricks.

- Make a border from paper cut into brick shapes, or by printing with a plastic or sponge brick.

- Provide samples of building materials, for example, a brick, tile, breezeblock, hinge and length of plastic guttering. Add a selection of books about buildings.

- Pin a length of string to each of the various parts of the house on the display, such as the walls, windows and doors, and then tie each string to the appropriate sample of material on the table below. Follow the strings from the display to the table and read the labels together.

- Label each part of the house and create freestanding card labels for the samples on the table.

- Supply magnifying glasses for children to observe the materials more closely, and writing materials for them to make drawings.

# Language and Literacy

- In a circle, pass around examples of building materials. (Use lightweight bricks for safety reasons.) Ask each child to say something about the material. What does it feel like? What might it be used for?

- Introduce the vocabulary associated with building a house, for example, 'brick', 'mortar', 'tile', 'hinge', 'window', 'frame', 'door', 'handle', and the words for different materials, such as 'plastic', 'wood' and 'metal'. Explain the uses of the various materials.

- Make a book about building a house using drawings, photographs and rubbings created by the children. Invite the children to attempt their own captions, or scribe for them.

- Set up a role-play estate agency with brochures from local agencies, photographs taken by the children and pictures cut from property magazines.

# Free Play

- Provide the children with different types of construction equipment so that they can build their own model houses. Display pictures of buildings and houses in various stages of construction to stimulate ideas.

- Include boxes of different sizes, along with 'small world' people and furniture, so that the children can develop imaginary play associated with building and furnishing a home.

# Mathematics

- Invite the children to take turns to stand against a brick wall and mark their heights with a piece of chalk. Ask them to estimate how many bricks tall they are and then check by counting.

- Make a model street with buildings created from recycled materials. Introduce mathematical language associated with size, shape and position, for example, point to the 'tall' spire with the 'round' clock face, 'on top' of the church. Number the houses and shops.

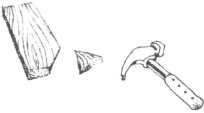

# Creative Work

- Supply appropriate recycled materials in the creative area, such as small and large boxes, alongside scissors, tape and glue so that children can make their own houses.

- Invite the children to paint pictures of their homes. Talkabout the features that need including, such as windows, doors and a roof.

# Our World

- Ask permission to take a group of children to visit a building site. Take photographs of houses in various stages of construction and talk to those involved, such as glaziers, plumbers, bricklayers and tilers.

- Visit an estate agency and collect brochures about houses for sale. Make comparisons between the size and shape of the buildings, and the types of materials used to build them.

- Examine building materials, such as plastic pipes, wooden doors, metal hinges and clay

or slate tiles. Talk about the need for materials to be strong to withstand extremes of weather conditions. What would happen if different materials were used, for example, paper walls and a cardboard roof? Devise simple experiments to test the materials.

# Outdoor Activities

- Make rubbings of the brick walls, fences and doors of surrounding buildings. Mount the rubbings on card and laminate them for protection. Take the finished cards outdoors and try to identify surfaces.

- Look for different patterns and shapes on the exterior of buildings.

## Home Links

- Invite a parent or carer from the building trade, or a keen DIY enthusiast, to come and talk to the children about the different stages of building or extending a house.

Ask parents or carers to:

- show their children photographs of different houses in the window of an estate agency.

# The Three Little Pigs

## Learning Intentions

- To use simple tools safely to construct two- and three-dimensional models.

- To join construction materials together using basic techniques.

## Starting Points

- Read or tell the traditional story 'The Three Little Pigs', and show the children samples of straw, sticks and bricks.

- Go for a walk to collect some twigs, and ask a pet owner or farmer for some straw.

## Display

- Create a border from short lengths of straw and sticks, and small bricks cut from textured wallpaper.

- Cut holes in the front and sides of an empty cereal box to represent doors and windows. Glue short lengths of straw to the front and sides of the box to create a house of straw. Leave the back clear to attach it to the wall display.

- Do the same to create a house of sticks, attaching small twigs using a combination of adhesive tape and glue.

- Glue small brick shapes from textured wallpaper onto a cereal box to represent the walls of the brick house. Add foil and brown paper to represent windows and a door.

- Staple the backs of the three houses in place on the wall display.

- Ask the children to suggest how they might create the three pigs and the wolf, for example, by painting, drawing or using collage materials. Encourage them to try out their suggestions and attach the finished pigs to the wall display.

- Invite the children to create three-dimensional models of the three pigs' houses using wooden or plastic bricks, sticks and straw and arrange these on a table below the wall display. Add a plastic pig in each house.

# Language and Literacy

- Sing the traditional rhyme 'This little pig went to market' and make a hand-shaped book together. Invite the children to draw or paint each pig, for example, 'going to market' or 'staying at home', and write the words of the rhyme underneath.

- Talk about how the pigs were afraid of the wolf to introduce a discussion about the children's own fears. Encourage all children to take part by giving them lots of praise for their individual contributions.

- Provide props and masks for dressing up as the three pigs and wolf, or dress up with the children and act out the story.

# Free Play

- Supply lots of different materials in a shallow sand tray alongside construction equipment, such as twigs, boxes, string, small stones, straw and sticks, to encourage the children to build shelters for farm, zoo or wild animals.

- Encourage the children to play freely with the items on the table display.

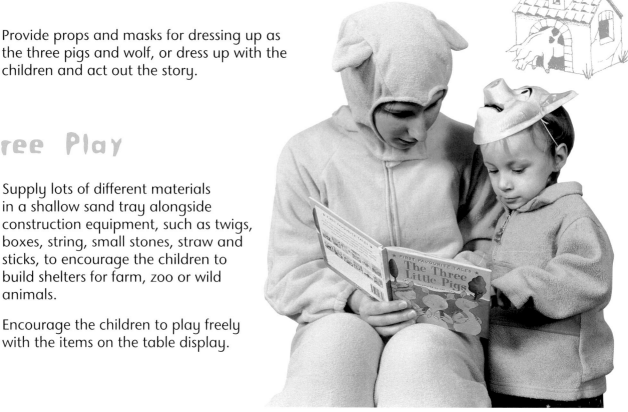

# Mathematics

- Create box models of the three pigs' houses and number the doors from 1 to 3. Cut a wide slot in each door and make ten envelopes from card, small enough to fit through the slots. Write a numeral from 1 to 3 on each envelope. Put the envelopes in a bag and invite the children to deliver them to the correct house. Then count the letters and talk about which pig has received the most letters, or the least.

- Read other traditional number stories, such as 'The Three Billy Goats Gruff' and 'The Three Bears', and introduce number rhymes, such as 'Five fat sausages' and 'Ten green bottles'. Accompany the stories and rhymes with props to encourage counting and number recognition.

# Creative Work

- Transform the role-play area into the pig's brick house. Include three pink fabric cloaks and three pig masks.

- Paint pictures of the pigs and wolf and use these paintings to retell the story.

# Our World

- Test the strength of the model houses. Is it easier to blow them over with a fan or a hair dryer?

- Talk about how the bricks made one house the strongest and explain how bricks are made by baking clay in a very hot oven. Try making bricks from clay.

- Visit a farm and find out what materials are used to build a barn, sheep pen, pig sty, dog kennel and hen house.

# Outdoor Activities

- Recreate the three pigs' houses by gluing straw to a sheet and draping it over a pop-up tent, building a tepee from long canes, and using full-size plastic or sponge bricks.

- Look at bricks in the environment. Are they all the same colour? Explore how different-coloured bricks are sometimes inserted to create patterns.

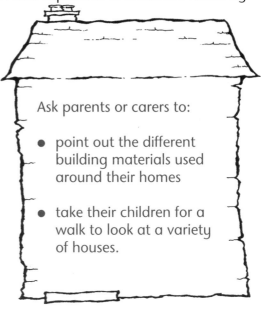

Ask parents or carers to:

- point out the different building materials used around their homes

- take their children for a walk to look at a variety of houses.

# Flying High

## Learning Intentions

- To be interested in how things work.

- To construct with a purpose in mind.

## Starting Points

- Visit the library, and borrow books about man-made flying machines. Look at the books together and talk about the children's experiences of flying.

- Visit a travel agency and collect brochures about holidays involving air travel. Invite the children to cut out pictures of different aeroplanes and glue these onto pieces of blue paper.

## Display

- Back a display board with blue paper and add clouds created by the children using paint and white fabric scraps.

- Make rockets, aeroplanes, helicopters and hot-air balloon models from recycled containers.

- Create a hot-air balloon from a blown-up balloon covered in strips of newspaper soaked in wallpaper paste. Allow to dry and then paint in bright colours.

- Attach the finished models to the display board, and suspend some in front as mobiles.

- Create a border from small, painted hot-air balloons cut from card.

# Language and Literacy

- Set up a role-play travel agency where children can browse through brochures and book holiday flights. Encourage writing and reading skills by including lots of print, and opportunities for writing.

- Invent stories about journeys in space and re-enact them. Use a pop-up tent as a rocket and cover a carpet area with cushions, draped in white sheeting, to represent the surface of the moon.

# Free Play

- Add model aeroplanes and helicopters to 'small world' equipment to encourage imaginary play.

- Set up a role-play aeroplane with rows of chairs so that the children can enjoy imaginary flights.

# Mathematics

- Attach a numbered card, from 1 to 10, to each child and ask them to imagine they are aeroplanes flying around the room. Choose a child to be in the control tower, calling out and holding up the numbers of the aeroplanes. When a child's number is held up he or she should fly in to land on the runway.

- Play rocket skittles. Make the skittles from plastic lemonade bottles and arrange them in a triangle, similar to tenpin bowling. Take turns to roll a ball at the rockets, knocking some over, then counting the skittles that are left.

# Creative Work

- Invite the children to imagine they are rockets flying through space to Handel's Royal Fireworks Music. Invent space noises using metallic objects, such as spoons tapped on pan lids, for added sound effects.

- Ask the children to paint pictures of aircraft. Mount them on brightly-coloured paper and surround the wall display with them.

# Our World

- Explain how gliders carry passengers on currents of air, and experiment with making gliders by folding pieces of paper.

- Make helicopter rotors using two strips of card pushed into a plastic straw at right angles. Try rolling the straw between the palms and releasing it to make it fly.

## Outdoor Activities

- Introduce large equipment, such as crates and planks, and create imaginary flying machines.

### Home Links

Ask parents or carers to:

- take their children to visit an airport to watch aircraft taking off and landing

- bring in holiday photographs of their children taken during flights to add to the display.

# Make it Move

## Learning Intentions

- To create a moving object from a selection of materials.

- To select the appropriate tools needed to shape, assemble and join materials.

## Starting Points

- Encourage the children to explore a selection of toys, which they can move by pulling strings, pushing wheels or turning handles and switches, such as string puppets, yo-yos, spinning tops, friction vehicles and a Jack-in-the-box. Talk about how the toys work, using appropriate vocabulary such as 'turn', 'switch', 'pull' and 'push'.

## Display

- Choose a low wallboard for the display so that the children can easily manipulate the models attached. Back the board in brightly-coloured paper.

- Make simple jointed puppets using card for the limbs, body and head. Join the various parts together with paper fasteners so that the puppets can be moved into different positions.

- Create faces with moveable eyes from large circles of card. Use collage materials for the features and cut out two holes for the eyes. Draw two eyes, the same size as the holes, on a strip of card. Attach the strip between two slots at the back of the card circle, so that the eyes appear through the holes. Move the strip of card from side to side to make the eyes move.

- Make 'Incy Wincy spider' from a small ball of black wool. Tie the end of the wool in a knot so that the ball cannot unravel, and add eight pipe-cleaner legs. Thread a length of wool through the tube and tie the top end to a cup hook glued above it. Fasten the wool spider to the other end and ask the children to pull the top end of the wool to make Incy Wincy spider move up and down the 'drainpipe'.

- Create a grandfather clock from boxes. Make a hole in the top of the clock, just below the clock face. Thread some wool through the hole and drop it down inside the clock face so that it emerges at the base. Stick on a pendulum. Paint a mouse, tie it to the other end of the wool and suspend it in front of the clock so that it moves. As the children pull the pendulum downwards, sing 'Hickory Dickory Dock' together as the mouse runs up the clock.

- Suspend a length of string across the display. Cut out a train shape from card and fasten two loops to the back of it. Thread the loops through the string so that the children can move the train backwards and forwards along the string 'track'.

# Language and Literacy

- Make paper plate faces and fasten a 'smiley' mouth made from card to the surface using a paper fastener. What happens to the facial expression when the mouth is turned upside down? Make a book with a similar moveable mouth on a face on the front cover and encourage the children to draw pictures and write about what makes them happy or sad.

- Use moving props to accompany favourite nursery rhymes, such as 'Jack and Jill' (bucket on a pulley system) and 'Little Miss Muffet' (spider on a string).

# Free Play

- Encourage children to make comparisons between a selection of friction-driven, battery-operated and free-wheel 'small world' vehicles. Talk about how each vehicle can be made to move.

- Explore how balls move along flat and sloping surfaces.

# Mathematics

- Make number spinners. Cut out a hexagon shape from card and divide it into six sections, numbered 1 to 6. Push a pencil through the centre of the spinner. Use the spinners for board games. Play simple number recognition games: spin the spinner and ask the children to read the numeral and do that many jumps, claps or hops.

- Use string to measure the distance travelled by small cars on different surfaces.

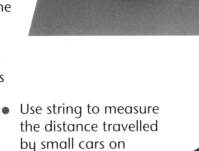

# Creative Work

- Encourage the children to imagine they are moving toys, such as a Jack-in-the-box, a remote-controlled car or a puppet on a string.

# Our World

- Experiment with creating pulleys and winches using recycled tubes and boxes, string and empty yoghurt pots.

- Make comparisons between the mechanisms of clocks that need winding up and those that are battery operated.

- Make a collection of moving toys, for example, wind-up models and spinning tops.

# Outdoor Activities

- Observe and discuss how pedal cycles work.

## Home Links

Ask parents or carers to

- talk to their children about how everyday tools and domestic appliances, such as drills and whisks, work.

# Useful Resources

There are many useful resources to enable children to extend their observation and investigation techniques. The following lists are for guidance and inspiration only, and are by no means comprehensive.

## Natural materials
- shells
- small stones and pebbles
- conkers, acorns, beech nuts, pine cones, sycamore and ash keys
- twigs and small logs
- pieces of wood
- leaves
- corks
- sponges

## Man-made materials
- paper, card and cardboard
- plastic sheeting, pipes, cartons and containers
- different man-made fabrics
- cellophane, foil and hologram paper

## Living things
- plants
- minibeasts
- fish
- watering cans, small garden tools, compost, plant pots, seeds and bulbs

## Resources for exploration and investigation
- magnifying glasses
- bug boxes
- funnels, clear flexible tubing, plastic pipes and connectors, jugs, sieves, whisks, water wheels, scoops and slotted spoons
- magnets
- colour paddles
- torches
- binoculars
- safety mirrors
- timers
- balances
- locks and keys
- cogs and gears
- nuts and bolts

## Resources for recording observations
- clipboards
- paper
- notepads
- writing tools
- cameras
- cassette recorder, microphone and tapes

## Resources to extend experiences and knowledge
- posters
- books
- computer programs
- video recordings
- scale models of living things

## Resources for safety
- goggles
- helmets
- woodwork aprons
- waterproof aprons